A Love Song for an Inked Doll

A book of Poetry & Prose

Words of Praise for A Love Song for an Inked Doll:

The Sweet Pinkham

"I am 100% in love with this book, it's the best fucking bo
ok ever!"

"Beautiful, Breathtaking and Swoontastic! It plays out like
a tragic love story with ups and downs so full of hope,
which makes it so hard to put down."

Azure

"A crack in the skull, in which one can see the vein
riddled grey matter churning pre-
apocalyptic montage of the ménage a trois,
man versus self versus woman often
concerned with both the visceral experience
and euphoric reflection of Love Lust Liquor and a Lady."

This book is dedicated to the woman who knows our history is already written across time and space. May some day you read this love song i wrote for you from my heart.

for the lads, rose city till i die!

A Love Song for an Inked Doll poetry & prose

first poem of 2010
there is redemption in that leap
the juxtaposition of b&w
yes no maybe go
soaking up all that is you tonight
sit here quietly
the muse effect
classic loud artistic exploration
you're like a dream
you in perpetuity
your skin like saran wrap
gravity orbitals
the storybook theory
sometimes excess is best in moderation
believe the storybook
hello, good night, goodbye & good morning beautiful
good morning beautiful
pools of joy
i know you are going too ...
i want us
burnt orange affair
u unrequited love from a barstool
i'm the radder
juxtaposition of opposites
the morning after ...
i am here for you
timbers ink & debauchery
can there be a tomorrow better than today
this is my way for you
your ink etched on skin like acrylics on fresh canvas
your silver lining
girls . love . excess . girls . love . divine
show me . tell me . fuck me
you are . i am . we can be
photographs on the wall
lift it . take it . love me
the excise of divinity
it is just you and me and all these strangers
tell me love one for you and i

not a single flower
with this love song
redheads, blondes, brunettes & bombshell hooligans
silence and exuberance are a visceral experience
the opposite of a rainbow
expressing my dissatisfaction
self absorbed aggrandizing hooligan
the ink pinup couple
tonight i say goodbye . tomorrow hello love
golden orgasms taste like chocolate
this love affair
a flower inside you
modern ink style
a story of you
more than the ink
like there is no tomorrow
beers like poems
i paint for you
as good as
under neon lights
of self evident prose
hoping i see you
pheromone wonderland kisses
as almost lovers
more to you
i know why
the latitude of our sunshine
i know what you did
joy match up
i wrote to you
to sleep next
just the bliss
dipole moments
there is tomorrow
all the nights

first poem of 2010

it's late February
with early spring sun
emily is playing in the yard
i am at the table
staring at tree's
they still have no leaves
i am alone here
the birds are singing
their love song to spring
i wish you were here
so i could sing
my love song to you
the girls playing and giggling
this sun is nice
warm for late February
so much hope
at the start of spring
emily keeps bringing me leaves from the rhodi
her gorgeous blue eyes
are glowing in the sun
so much wonder and awe
how gently we are
in this silence
my soul longs to express
for you
i keep thinking
their is redemption in that expression
for me it is
the release of love
so long bottled and beaten back
from neglect
for you it is the acceptance
of love
so long withheld from cruel lovers
i want your hand to hold mine
your heart to fill
with a love for the ages
this overflowing bounty

is the story of us
redemption is ours for the taking
as am i
for the action and refrain
you only need to show me
your heart is open
you desire the capacity
to express the deep capacity
of your heart bursting with love
i seek only a way to express
my grand love for life
a safe place to seek refuge
from the cruel world that sucks
my positive energy
emily is sitting next to me now
in this warm sun
she wants me to read her this poem
to write more about her
beautiful eyes
she says its nice to love someone
you feel so nice
the sun feels wonderful
in this late February moment
listening to the birds sing
their love song to spring
i wish you were next to me
the kids singing in the yard
playing and giggling
such hope in this day
i want to sing
a love song to you
that warms your soul

there is redemption in that leap

i write to forget
i write to remember
all my words are some thing
i cannot tell you
if i could say them
would you smile or laugh
or just walk away
could you love me today
tomorrow
or in that moment
we first kiss
i already am
you must believe in something
that has never existed
for you in me
who has never watched
it stay
there is redemption in that leap
so take my hand
trust what you cannot see
feel to believe that tomorrow
we can both love
without fear of pain
i can only promise you i am worth it
promises are not worth salt
if we do not act
i wonder if you will even give me a chance
to love you for who you are
i can fill your heart
with a love you have dreamed of
if only you will open the door
let me in as i
sing this song of you in spring
in hope you can just hear my words
feel their truth
i see something in you
the perfect balance to me

the juxtaposition of b&w

i sit here tonight a couple of days removed
from the most perfect weekend
a couple of days prior
to what feels like redemption
the passage of an anniversary
that can no longer have any meaning
or power in my life.
i sit here thinking only of the future
knowing the past has no power
though it has given me all the lessons
all the smarts one can hope for
i wonder what you think
if you could ever believe
in something so grand as futures untold
sometimes in the moments of joy
i feel my most alone
like right now
i fear what is not quite mine
right as you reach for it
it vanishes
this moment will pass in time
make its way back again
i know this
because my cycle of time
i cannot predict
i want to love you
for reasons i cannot fully write
in black and white
i have changed again from where i was
these changes all
led me to you
some dream of redemption
a life of celebration
balance those things we share

yes no maybe go

the answer is seven!
i never saw any yellow or purple
i win!
i saw some brilliant shit
no i saw . . .
that is love
it's always for love
a day i know
i let my friends down
a day i know
they love me more than ever
this day has so many conflicting emotions
today is over
tomorrow will be something else
i cannot explain
i have seen a day similar
well
at least there are reactions
they are similar
it's going to be hard
to say what i feel
since this mixed emotion
has so many conflicting statements
i love you
my friends
my lovers
i love you
i cannot follow you down
this rabbit hole tonight
the night that is over
i cannot chase you down this rabbit hole
because i love you
because i love me
this is more than i can express to you
because i see you
are not ready to hear me
this is as it should be.
tonight, that is past

is the end to something
i had no control over
a dream i tried to create
with no merit
i am not a miracle worker
i know this
i tried a long time ago
with someone oblivious of me
i love you
yes i do!
that is all there is to say . . .
i cannot be tonight
what you want or need
because this is confusion
you are me and i am you
azure says what is next?
what is it we create
beyond what you cannot see
i say it is all what it is
i love you
i love you
because i know you cannot
know we cannot meet
i failed my friends tonight
yet they love me none the less!

soaking up all that is you tonight

the clarity of an event
knowing you are the sum of the parts
is sometimes more than you want
i do not wish to be anywhere else but here near you
it is what i want more than the sleep i crave
it is more than the world i crave
because it is this love which is i
this tiny capacity is not more than today
i cannot see what is next
this belongs to a moment in time
i see where the past belongs to a memory
too much whiskey
too much Jamesons in the moment
too much
its not yet futbol season
i wish i was in the terraces with you
singing those drunken songs
i cannot believe in this feeling
without it running all around me
maybe because i want to more than ever
maybe because this space won't let me
come on baby flash me your smile
come on baby say you can love me
come on tell me something famous tonight
tell me what is right
cause i am in la la land
like there is no tomorrow
come on say you know me tonight
i love your vans, i love your red
in those fishnets and your punk skirt
it is something i have waited for my entire life
all my life to know
you are no different than me
i am just soaking this up tonight
soaking up all that is you
i wish i could see straight tonight
i want to believe in our future tonight

sit here quietly

well hello, maybe i am not ready to ride
yesterday, with its crazy i cannot go this way vibe
is not so clear an uncertain wave
i like being alone
except when i do not
then i feel anxious
i almost made the wrong choice last night
riding a bike is easy
they say you never forget the feel
so long in this last year i denied myself
an opportunity to ride
before that, someone took away my opportunity
used it as a weapon against me
yet, riding is something ingrained in my very nature
it is my pleasure regulator, mood stabilizer
last night, being melancholy for the fact
i cannot have what i want
the patience to do this right
i was searching for a place
of comfort to ride the angst away
like a sixth sense it is not hard to find
you might be happy to know
after all that work
i sat alone in the studio
just could not bring myself to stoop so low
i realize i may not be ready
for all the promise you bring
the trouble with knowing you can do anything
is sometimes you forget
what you cannot do until the aftermath engulfs you
i am not always a patient man
even if the reward is great
the ironic fact of having waited my entire life
for the two things i am the best at
having only participated partially in one
i dare to dream of the second
i should just sit here quietly till you take my hand

the muse effect

sometimes when you ask for what you want
the universe answers with an overabundance of love
sometimes it is a little much to know
six years i have bottled up
the true connection to my well of emotion
six years of recrimination
nothing resembling love
it is always the form of the muse which connects
the well of emotion to a love of something red
this bright color fireball of orange yellow red delight
you, my muse
it was not even a starting place to open this door
you kicked it open when we sat and talked
after so long in isolation
for some weeks after that fall day
when you were wicked hung over and i was so scattered
i had this thought of warmth
i traced back in my memories
all the times we shared
i am not often giddy
those thoughts run around the air
still some time had to pass
before i traced their origin to the well
i was able to pry the cork off with one statement of hope
i need my well to show you how to love
give me this opportunity
my emotional connection to creativity
has been on a high ever since
these words flow like endless water reigning down
sparks of creativity driving me
red muse is the color of new beginning

classic loud artistic exploration

i dreamed of you last night
the ever present love song of desire
you are a pure melody to me
those first strokes as the tune begins
i dreamed of us last night
in the cool spring air
after a day in the sun
with laughter and joy
i dreamed of you last night
your smile etched in my mind
your eyes a smile i can see
being lost for some time in
i dreamed of us last night
the first touch of skin to skin
a light brush on the arm
fingertips dancing on the small of the back
i dreamed of you last night
the scent of your pheromones linger
like a scrumptious thought
to lay my head upon
i dreamed of us last night
of the very beginning of love
of first kisses that taste
of delicious strawberries
i dreamed of you last night
i dreamed of us

you're just like a dream

these words keep flowing onto paper
with ease
as if already written in my soul
i keep smiling and writing
thinking of you sitting
with your legs curled
under you
reading them from the couch
a wry smile as you wondered
is this kat for real
the muse effect
is such a wonderful state of energy
a little bit less than perfect bliss
bliss is always the next step
when offered up as a path to redemption
with these words come images and wonderment
of warm summer days in the future
girls laughing and giggling together in the sun
picking flowers and bringing them to us
as we lay in soft green grass
of cold winter nights
on the couch in front of a fire
talking of tomorrows dreams
for little girls growing older
the warmth of the blanket
like a spotlight on our love
happiness is ever present in waking thoughts
that may never come to fruition
how i dream of you and your mystery
a comfort to my energy
i know me so well
you, i want to know well
will that smile be my comfort and redemption
will it be an anthem of unspoken longing
i am not sure i should care how this ends
when i know no one can recognize me and stay
other than i feel the promise

of a storybook love
the promise of redemption in a life
wrapped up in the comfort of strangers
where i have manufactured
all that you see
from this gaping hole
i can feel the pain in your soul
from those past stories
i can see your reserve
the mystery you bring
i am not those men
i am a capable redemption
a storybook love
is what i am designed for
the everlasting belly
of uncertainty
cannot contend
with my eternal well
of optimism
for it is
a fundamental love
so rooted in faith
believe in me
you will be rewarded
love me
you will find
your beloved happiness
is a storybook
of redemption
happy girls growing laughing and loving

you in perpetuity

there is this feeling i cannot shake tonight
i know this one so well
having been here before
so much conflicting emotions in me
go here, go there
i can see how the field plays
it is nights like these that are so tough to get through
so worth the reflection tomorrow
i am sorry to always take you down this path
my friend (to self) there is tomorrow
yet i sometimes cannot choose
any other path to walk
at least we have done it before
we know how this ends
i am yours till the bitter end
we can see a field of games and play
you are my endeavor
i love you like no other
i knew after some fucked up words
i needed to get drunk
the eventual end of a manic session
words words words just flow like a river
created from the rain
i wonder, this bar stool is it a place
we can remember each other
is it a place
you remember
we can love each other
i just want to know
there may be a chance
tomorrow, next week
any time, any time
is there just five minutes we can spend
i want to tell you all i am
i want to hear all you are
we cannot do it in five minutes

will you give it to me
we must start somewhere
you can absolutely think
you are going no where
then "bam!"
you are where you need to be
your world is complete with a pearl
love me beautiful
i can be your pearl
in this crazy turbulent life
i can be so much more
than you can imagine
if you let me
will you let me love you like i dream
like i know you need me too
there is no end to the way i can express this
which means there is no end to how i can love you
just take that step forward
embrace what you have always wanted
what you have never experienced
let me love you beautiful
this night, where you are not here
is a night i cannot forget
i wish i can remember
i wish you were here
for an outcome
i want to remember
how to love you
i want to know
how you respond to love
i want to celebrate
your soul
kiss your smile love
your beautiful smile
surrounded by
those mystery pool eyes
i can be lost in those gorgeous eyes
for forever and a day

your skin like saran wrap

it's that time of summer
standing
on the right side of the road
the warmth
wrapped around your skin
like Saran wrap
small beads of sweat
trickle down your back
just the thought of cool suds
brings us a smile
i can hear
the girls laughing
i can feel
you smiling at me
my instinct
is to reach out
for you
i feel you
slide up
my hand
on your back
wiping a drop
from your skin
a purr
i look in your eyes
those dark luscious eyes
their mystery
you lean in
our lips spark
that familiar fire
how i love
your heat
in this summer sun

gravity orbitals

can do you go wild
been running around
all hours of the night
stumbling in and out of bars
drunk happy melancholy
thinking through
so many different thoughts
thinking through
so many different situations
wondering if
there is anything pertinent to say
wondering if
you have anything to say
at all
i am this bright shining ball
of light
fire
flying through space
at speeds well past
the speed of light
attracted to your mass
of reserved love
this giant gravity
pulled me in so close
will my entropic energy
force a sling shot affect
as your calming water
looks to douse my fire
will gravity set an orbit
you and i can reach
each other from

the storybook theory

someday next week
these revelations will sink in
maybe i will not be so melancholy
maybe i will finally sleep
remember a few weeks ago
all was as perfect as could be
the hope of a chance
so many future stories
untold
i always stumble
just as i begin my stride
i was sort of hoping
the opposite theory
held weight
i know as a scientist
an avid purveyor
of chaos theory
the simple knowledge
choices we make
far outweigh the consequences
of pheromones and biochemistry
sometimes
you hit a single
then get tagged at second
sometimes its three strikes
you're out
rarely is the storybook
a home run
when i remember
to look
in my history
of chemical reactions
i see the storybook
is a classic tragedy

sometimes excess is best in moderation

i saw this moment in my afternoon
i new i was manic
there was no going back
for an instance i had the flash
of all the events of the last two months
two years, two decades that led
to this uncontrolled exuberance
still the next day
i do not regret
my excess
i do fear pure creativity
the pure moment of lust in energy
it will tear me apart if i give in to it
if i forget it should not control me
as if riding a bike and letting go of the handle bars
down a hill knowing you will crash
accepting that the wind rushing through your hair
your smile is pure energy
maybe with your arms out
this is as close to flying as may come
i drank my jamesons to say goodbye to you
to say goodbye to me in that time
now that time is over however short
or long it has really been
i can only loose myself once in reckless abandon
really only when there is something to loose myself in
my story, this story i keep writing, rewriting
is one of tragic melancholy heartache
for each moments of pure bliss that just slipped away
it is true people only like you when you are up
for every up an equal part down
two times in between
my chaos, my joy, is the perfect path around a circle
a cycle continually changes
the juxtaposition of shadow and light
i see the moment of loss
when i look down at my hands trembling

believe the storybook

shaking in that energy state
i thought of you
all the promise i felt
all the hope of beginning again
when you want to know
tomorrow is worth your time today
i have this beautiful knack
suspending my disbelief
simply believe the storybook ends
any different than i know
tomorrow is always a joy
if you see
something to pursue
it is pure bliss
when that pursuit
comes right back
chases you back
all of my life i have waited
for my story book
to speak feel love the universe
i am
so i sacrifice today
for a hope of tomorrow
that is unrequited
my art is my love
my daughter is my love
my words are my love
my science is my love
i can still hear her voice
an audible hallucination while creating
the warmth of my favorite september evenings
her voice full of the love i crave
"i know what you are doing
i love you lucas"

hello, good night, goodbye & good morning beautiful

the crescent moon rises as the night started with a hug
a brief hello and it was apparent
you were happy to see me
oh that smile is so beautifully intoxicating
i met you with a smile of my own
felt deep in my soul
a hello you could bank on
as the night rolled on in that dark bar
with the streams of people all around us
this cacophony of voices a mass of punk humanity
our eyes and smiles met on many an occasion
awash in that sea of mass
never really keeping a conversation
except through those subtle communications
i could feel inside our parallel track
this physical pheromone a biochemical reaction
i sit here across the table watching you watching me
watching you talk through all these masses
your beauty is breath taking in this environment
of beers and cheers and the noise of bar life
i am just here to be present for you
to soak up your life your friends
i love the comfort of strangers
tonight i will stand apart for you to see
i can feel your ink and your eyes upon me
as we finally find ourselves next each other
you lean in to make a comment
that look in your eyes that says you know
its time to go and i am coming with you
i want to touch those milky pools
in your eyes as you stare at me
your smile is gorgeous in this light
i have butterflies every time you look at me
i wonder what it might be like

good morning beautiful

no i dare not say, but then you look at me again
somehow i know what to do
somehow i want to touch you
like soft brush strokes on canvas
tracing the ink on your skin
a moment to share the way
i want to care for your heart
caress your soul to remember
what it is like to know passionate love
you have never met a kat like me
you may never know
i can express
this love for you
there is that second when you stare
eyes like deep pools
can you feel me here in this dark place?
where love is all i want to know of you
where my care is knowing
you may never be any different around me
your skin so close to my touch
your ink a love song i may never know
can you feel this longing?
feel this love
i stand here waiting to give you
then you give me that look that says lets go
i instinctively know what to do
good morning beautiful
its five am
i do not want to say goodbye

pools of joy

pure joy is a high before the fall
i could hear the door click shut
you were there in front of me
hello beautiful!
your smile a wonderful light
as you walked up to me
your smell intoxicating
this time as it was the first
inhale
i can feel upon my skin
a remembrance of why
i have loved you since the day we met
you smile again as we embrace
your body an insinuation to me
those luscious lips a delicious reminder
of what is to come next
i breathe deep your touch
the gentle reminder of a love not lost
you must be strong to tame a manic soul
divine to love one like me
your touch is a sensuous delight
as your fingers run through my hair
tracing their way down my cheeks
to my lips, another soft kiss
the smile warms my soul
your eyes are pools of joy
i want to stare in forever and a day
when you touch me i feel love
when i touch you i know love
i am love, i give love to you
eternal words combined
my fingers caress your skin
the small of your back where my art resides
delicious ink i am going to explore in you
for this love forever
for this waking dream
of you and i here so very long ago

i know you are going to . . .

i keep walking these city streets
wondering if you are ever going to talk to me
wondering if you are ever going to write to me
of the love that i feel in my heart
or of the love i want
i wish you were here with me
though as these city streets pass
i can feel the distance between us
a distance so great i could break
i know there is this story of life
a heartache in tragedy
this story is only a story that is lived
never written in stone
yes doll
i can love you for you
i wonder if you can love me for me
i keep stumbling in and out of bars
and back home again
i wish you were here with me
on the couch with your head on my lap
your gorgeous eyes staring up at me
all our words floating on joyous whispers
in the electric space between us
yet sitting here as i am
the dark of night has crept in
the silence of sitting here alone
could i deserve more than this silence
more than just a few words
or a touch of your skin
i may never feel your piercing gaze again
as those milky eyes are pools of joy
in the parchment of my dreams
sitting here with my heart in my hand
i wish you were here with me love
to wash away these thoughts from sinking in
you are going to break my soul
for all the ages to read our storybook

i want us

my best bukowski from a barstool
the cue on balls
as the soul blues begins
i am back in the garden
where magic always finds me
luscious ladies and the like
in the darkness that is the bottom for some
a fresch klesch untarnished
by the dirt and grime of gutter affairs
this type of debauchery is for pleasure
nothing else, unless the current is right
we never really can say
where we will end
i am so very quiet inside
first time in some while
as this mania feels like its been on me forever
energy can be fun and useful
also very destructive
what else do you have
to say tonight
in the din of dusk and video poker
i want to say so much
i hope i get to see you tonight
yet this conversation is always really with myself
i am here cause i like to watch
its my art to write or capture that which i see
in you, in me, what i want to say is us
what i want to be, is us
what i want to feel is you, is love, is us
i always lead with the heart until i do not
you always wear yours on your sleeve
somehow i think that makes us so very similar
i feel i will never know, yet beautiful, for you, for me
for a shot at a beloved future
i will forever try to be worthy of you
endeavor to the love i bring you or we will never start
i want us to believe

burnt orange affair

i can usually see the path in the street
tonight the concrete leads me to Kelly's
back to where i first met you
back to where i first fell in love with you
a love song for an inked doll
that is what i write for you, for me
for an opportunity that is us in a future
not quite defined - no expectations
that is the rule of a stable mania
melancholy and joy is what comes
with expectations
sitting again on a bar stool
i cannot define
i cannot see more than three feet in front of me
not because i am blind, but because what else is there
beyond this brittle space
this stool and the warm beer, cold women
you know Waits knows it so well
barfly's and hipster's, bohemians till the end
i saw that LA was no better than my beloved rose city
but portland is better than anywhere else i have been
anywhere else i want to be
this city has you, it has me
it can and loves to celebrate us
no expectations, no regrets
i can still feel this melancholy
so i write to forget
just like i drink to remember
so it goes for the poet and artist who lives in mania
my life is always this burnt orange affair
an episode of some day time special where the kid
we all want to win, perpetually lost in tragedy
the punk in me says "ah FUCK it"
you are a hottie and that is what i need
the comfort of a stranger to swim in for awhile
i live in the day for those moments in the night
its one of the only places i fit in this affair

unrequited love from a barstool

a love song for an inked doll
these words my confessional
pheromones make the whores moan
so says the bohemian chemist
a sex kitten next to me
no love
i have no taste
for this skirt chasing anymore
there is no joy
in the penchant for the divine
where i used to love
the pursuit
now it bores my soul to death
i am so desperately sad
for this thought
which pervades a melancholy
when my new paints come in
i will not go out for months
all those canvas' to express
my love
unrequited love from a barstool
the companion volume
to a love song
i am such a cynical fuck
for all these words i write
that's a fucking yummy white russian
he poured for the old man next to the soda water
maybe i am just old
in doing this
playing games
for all the little hipsters
just barely old enough
to hold a drink
laughing
i love this mockery and melancholy
it pervades my punk soul
i was born of a cynic in a time

midway through the post sixties love fest
before my dad
loaded bombs on planes
body bags off helos
it was the opposite of hippie love
you are a doll!
do you know
in the absence of anything else to say
i will refer to day one of our meeting
just keep pissing it away
this storybook you always write
as a tragedy
hannah says the words should flow
as i love your ink
my night flashback is complete
i do not feel so sad anymore
enough beer and a pretty lady
in conversation
are enough
to forget all this melancholy
i am going to talk to you
after i smoke
so says B to the chemist
my kind of doll
for she is the same crazy
as me
this is the debauchery
of my life
oh, the first fishnets
of the night
thank you
for this dream
only the Olympian
can bring

i'm the radder

one morning many years ago i got off the train
at pioneer plaza and started walking up past The Guild
my head was hung low like so many days before
staring at that concrete i kept walking
spirits as low as they could be
in my dark hole where the sun never shines
i did feel love
a manic man like me
for every high is a low
i am as bright as a deep dark hole
where the sun doesn't shine
the high yellow moon hidden
behind gray scale skies
until i stood on the corner
watching this white vintage car
roll up the street slowly like a god drive by
the dali lama sat in the back seat
his hand hanging out the window
he looked right at me
smiled then waved
as he rolled on like a god drive by
my soul, my hole of darkness
was soon filled with light
my head picked up my heart
filled with eternal love
my smile stretched ear to ear
i still feel that divinity today when
i see that image roll by
the dali lama smiled on me
in a beloved rose city morning
when i needed love more than anything else
i am the radder
for existing here in your life
you should reach out and see
how the high yellow moon
comes out to play

juxtaposition of opposites

the silver lining in the midst of darkness
i was sitting on the front stairs
listening to the rain in the night
i do not seem to sleep to much anymore
sometimes i do not even try
i can feel again, and that is enough for now
i am creative again
connected to my emotional core
i have you to thank for that
i have love to dream about
i have a life to live, somehow
this is why i cannot sleep
my life is settled and unsettled
always this juxtaposition of opposites
the rain smells so warm
i smile to think of you
i long to smile at you, touch you, love you
sitting here in the dark of my porch
in the comfort of no light
i am reminded of the old adage,
"you pay your money and you take your chance
when dealing in love and romance"
this is the silver lining in it all
its a gamble with Vegas odds
i cannot expect to beat Vegas odds
maybe i can sleep knowing i cannot win with you
i have this picture
i hope there is a love in you
as great as i can imagine

the mornings after . . .

the mornings after you visit my dreams
i wake up to this feeling you were there
with me in that comfort of white sheets
as the warm sun rises and rustles us from our slumber
i always long to feel your body insinuated next to mine
your skin as soft as morning sun
the scent is our love
as i trace the ink along your skin with soft fingertips
till your beautiful smile greets me with warm love
the morning sun lighting our eyes
this is the dream the morning after
yet this love
i woke feeling
all my poetic license are just
words someone else will read
and your heart will not hear
you visited my dreams last night
with the flurry of a fiery red maelstrom
for the things i have yet to do
i know what is coming
what i am about to choose
i awake this morning to that same warm yellow sun
on white sheets i wish i shared with you
yet love, this poetic license
is it winning your heart with words?
or as you are off in a world outside of here
is the distance and silence between us
greater than my words can span
i want your heart and soul
the warm summer sun shines
on our love
write this storybook affair
with all these smiles and sunshine
yeah, i was about to change it up mid-stream
till i went for a walk and remember that
i like myself the way i am
i like how i feel right now
with all these smiles and sunshine

i do not need to love you
i want too
i want to be loved by you more
it does not even seem possible
maybe i will admit to the wind
i like it better that way
no real complications to hinder the way
i feel about you
about me
yeah, it is kind of ironic to admit
i am almost perfect this way from afar
i need this emotional center
these words as much as i want you
but love, something you do not know of me
i am the rare breed you read about
watch on the silver screen
i am that wonderful exception to the rule
of a hard knock life
i cannot be any clearer when i say
you must choose
me and this storybook life
you must endeavor to be rare too
yeah, i have this wondrous smile for the thought
it has been such a long time without the sheets
and joy of those explorations
i may go back to chasing skirt
if you don't come around
i need this creativity for art
instead of wasted on
saturation
i thought you would understand
who and what i was
for that is what i desire
in our storybook
our love affair
for the ages

i am here for you

oh my joy for you love
is a night i remember we spent
till the wee hours of the next day
when normal folks are just getting up
we were heading home in different cabs
i remember the whole night in vivid detail
your smile on me so warm to my heart
it started with a hug and joy
like seeing me for the first time in months
i liked your touch and was so happy inside
you insisted i join your table
so i sat across from you
to watch you, to smile at you
oh my joy for you love
it grew that night
as we kept drinking and celebrating
celebrating your life
i am a stranger here amongst your friends
yet, love, that night i could see your joy
reflected back at me
i think you know why i am here
i am here for you, for love
so when it was time to move on to the next stop
it did not surprise me to be going with you
the joy of maybe being your toy
buzzed euphoric in the backseat
our mouths just talking
i reached out to rub your arms
touch your inked skin
i just wanted you to feel my love
i just wanted a moment alone
on to the bar for another Jamesons
feeling a little heady
wondering how it would end

timbers ink and debauchery

round and round spinning
till there is no end
i like it when
wednesday's are thursday's
and thursday's are friday's
its your hump day
before beer & debauchery
capped off with the timbers
drunk singing
i smile at how i am going to erase
this blot of frustration and inconsistencies
i am already in a good mood today
for the hope my friday evening
may consist of sex drugs
the timbers
your friday is surely to follow up
with the same for me
i am all smiles and joys
i know how to forget
i cannot love you
i cannot even talk to you
your silence is my blessing
to free me
of this false hope you instilled
let's get on with the real joy
of a storybook that drips of love
as much as it does
of ink and debauchery
which so characterizes
my artistic life

can there be a tomorrow better than today

been staring at these photographs so long
i sometimes long for someone to look at me
the way my models look at the camera
i long for you to look at me that way
with love adoration and care
i have these pictures of you
looking at my camera
you are not looking at me
i long for someone to look at me like that
fill my soul with her love
express my love for you
i have been thinking of you
in the early morning hours
when the darkness is so black
i am drunk from all this beer
the comfort of strangers
can only go so far love
from this bar stool where i write
i write pretty words
take pretty photographs
paint pretty acrylics
all for this one chance
to express something that moves you
i have been staring at these photographs for so long
i long for you to look at me this way

this is my way for you

this thing
is always the same
how it ends with me and you?
i always laugh
at myself
finding me here
in the garden
where magic always seems to happen
i love you
if that is not clear
when asked tonight
who a love song for an inked doll is for
i can only say you know her
it is for everyone
i chuckled when she said
that was the best answer
i never really thought
i was being anything
other than coy
never thought that was right
i am a pimp
in this world of junkies
the astute words can only come
from a chemist like me
i know i love for all that is
your inked nature
the debauchery of this life
makes me smile
more than anything
in this world
like when the crowd cheers
for a delicious doll
as she takes off her clothes
or the Timbers in a 3-nil shellacking
i see no difference in the two
it is just my personality
of controlled chaos
in this night life

of denizens, harlots and observers
i am definitely
the watcher
in this world of wonder
can you love me like that?
is it something
beyond your recognition
i am in love with you doll
isn't it obvious
i keep trying to show you
in what i do not think
is so subtle
give me more of a reason
to love you doll
i can see here now
you cannot
i want you to know
i can
this night
in its genesis
is so very full
of non sequitor beginnings
in what it is
i have no say about
your love of me or lack there of
i cannot see me waiting for
i cannot see me being this very life
to you
i want to love you
for all that you are
for all that you can be
in this era of inked dolls
alternative lives
my magical rose city
my beloved rose city
is full of pure joy
when the sun shines
my way for you

your ink etched on skin like acrylics on fresh canvas

the same place
in a different time
plays the same tune we
all melodically flow along too
you move with its vibe
a soul beyond expression
this soul lives on
forever
i can see why i capture
that layer of light upon the skin
so soft and subtle
a hue cast
in this red glaze effect
the garden is just a clank and chime
away from the poker
your skin in this hue
is so much more than divinity
your ink etched on skin
like acrylics on fresh canvas
the shadow detail of light
this red wavelength can project
i came here again to write
to see what i am creating from the light
always in the filter of blue
i can crystallize
from within this faded haze
more shades than high key lighting
the epoch of summer sun
when you find yourself
in my beloved rose city
the ink and skin intoxicating
black boots and fishnets
under red dark room lights
this amber hue
a wavelength of the heart
it is my bohemian art
the touch most sensual
as the beat keeps

its cadence of a manic soul
i can call these words a love song
you can call it this night
as the light falls on inked skin
a high key note
of rambling blues
this worship
with denizens and characters
who have a defined soul
they are the stuff of stories
the energy of my creation
i love the dirty hipster
the punk
my inked dolls
whose skin are like acrylic canvas'
i have yet to paint
everything is the nature i have yet to create
this perpetual moving boat, cast adrift
on choppy oceans
i am but a notion
of the wind
whispered from your luscious lips
in this wondrous red hue
i am always trying to capture
with or without you love
the candle light flickers
shadows on wooded tables
we see a light left longer
a light that burns
of love and passion
i want you
accept me
this light
it shines on us too

your silver lining

i am your silver lining
it was quite clear last night
when i saw you
that whatever had passed
had changed your mind
i had that moment of joy
tinged with the thought
what to do next?
maybe i was really winning
you with my words
when i had no other choice
i am your silver lining
because i always forgive
i will never forget
that this is love
for us to grow into
i was going to give up on you
till you smiled at me last night
as you sought me out
that warmth from your body
next to mine
your scent an intoxicant
for the rest of the night
i do not recall much beyond that
just a scent and a smile
your lips whispering in my ear
i am sorry love
i am your silver lining

girls . love . excess . girls . love . divine

i was sitting in the sun
watching the clouds play
thinking of you
the day we walked in
the warm summer sun
your skin supple from the moist heat
we stopped at that quaint place by the water
drank some cold beers
talking for hours
as we stared in each others eyes
i would drop a bead of cold
condensation from my bottle
on your shoulder and trace its path
along your ink
so delicious was your smile
your eyes a pool of milky love
i could feel our exploration
all the souls divine
we just laughed and drank
the warmth of the summer sun
you remember that old couple
who came by and said we were perfect
in love with the divine
i just smile knowing your love
my love, our love
was an afternoon in summer sun
when everyone smiled upon us
you would touch my arm
i would look over at your smile
those luscious lips
a fiery kiss
all the love our souls divine

show me . tell me . fuck me

sipping on this beer
sitting at the end of the bar
the bohemian sitting next to me
a man of some fifty years of age
threw me a curve
when he asked me if i had met my love?
i responded with yes and was about
to tell a storybook tale till he
cut me off and said
did she tell you she loved you?
yes
did she show you she loved you?
pause, yes
did she fuck you?
of course!
in that order?
well, no
we fucked first
then she said she loved me
and finally she showed me she did
he smiled a wry smile
asked me simply
how do you know
she is your love?
when the order is so wrong
opposite of a storybook

you are . i am . we can be

standing on this corner
in the midnight black
of a drunken night
i reached out to take your hand
as you began to walk away
you smiled that beautiful smile
your eyes glowing sparkles
in the dark night
we were with your friends
i know i am not supposed to show
all my affection for you
i did not want you to just walk off
without you feeling
you are the bright light
in my dark night
which fires my soul to be creative
i am the perfect companion
to your attraction
for these late night antics
of music beer and debauchery
i am the love you have never seen
we can be the perfect match
partners in crime for our evenings
if you would just let me in
on this street corner
acknowledge for your friends
that smile, this touch, is the start
of what the historians will write
as a love affair for modern times
you are more than my creative muse
right here love
you are all i want to touch
right here doll
you are who i do not want to see walk away
without stealing a touch
maybe a kiss

photographs on the wall

just a another hump day
the dirty old man loves
the middle of the week
with its connotations
he sits on his porch
like i sat
on the balcony in the loft
the dolls a parade
on the street
happy is the nostalgia
sitting and smoking fat zags
those warm summer days
a delight to experience
like the night we spent
laying in the grass
staring at the stars
talking about the clouds
hand in hand arm to arm
skin to skin
on warm summer nights
i have these memories
like photographs on the wall
your beautiful voice an allure
our fingers entwined
as stars dance for us
with your skin
a wonderful brush
on my arm
the warm air
smooth in the light
of a memories glow
your lips kiss my skin
with a drunk desire
to express a punks love
after a night drinking flirting fun
we are here laying in the grass
holding hands like school kids
i have no clue what time it was
i really didn't want this to change

i loved waking up to you
after that wondrous night
under the stars
your head nuzzled on my chest
your leg curled on me
the sun creeping up in the east
i kissed your forehead
not wanting a moment to stop
your love so deep in me
a touch of the divine
gently tracing my fingers
along your ink
supple canvas
i waited for your eyes
to open
so i could swim
in your milky pool
caress the love
i can feel in your touch

lift it . take it . love me

in a day
in an hour
in a minute
i can go up and down
a weight
a relief
then euphoria and tragedy
i want to be near you
to lift this weight i feel
i want to touch you
to keep this joy i feel
i need you to love me
to balance this energy
of bundled emotions
you evoke in me
oh joy
oh euphoria
can we love like no other?
oh weight,
oh tragedy
can we love each other?

the excise of divinity

sometimes the nights are just as solid
as the days when we found only sun
the linguistics of the night
are very direct and vocal
as those mid afternoon sessions
drinking in each other
tonight though, i can feel you watching me
every time i look at you
you make eye contact then look away
i try to smile but i feel it is just a grimace
maybe it is clear
to you or your friends
that now there is no silence
in this cacophony of bar noise
with all of your friends watching us
i am a little to drunk to be focused
i can feel this shadow
falling on my thoughts
the euphoria of the evening
eaten away by the disjointed nature
our way of relating
tomorrow will be different
if not a tiny bit the same
all i really want
is to be in love with you
where mornings we wake
to the saturation of each others skin
afternoons spent in laughter
the joy of girls playing in summer sun
where evenings are spent
exploring the pleasure
that love exudes in you and i

it is just you and me and all these strangers

we are sitting in this semi circle booth
my show is all around us
the fans are all around us
as the band keeps playing
a raucous tune
all these people keep talking
talking to me and you
as we sit nestled in this corner
drinking in each other
for a second it is just you
and me here in the silence
of the noise of the club
you whisper you love me
i steal a nibble on your neck
then a kiss
all these strangers around us
pause and watch
a pair as unique as us
so obvious in love
its just you and me
and all these strangers
the show continues to praise
the art you helped me create
the love we are here to celebrate
the show plays on as the band rocks
this love song for you
my beloved inked doll
with luscious skin of acrylic canvas
eyes of milky pools
the dolls want to be you
it is just you and me
and all these strangers
watching us flirt
watching us love
until its last call and the final notes stumble out
just you and me and this love song

tell me love

of a sensational time
i turned around at the familiar touch
your hand on my back
that beautiful smile
as i turned to stare in your eyes
oh dear i did not expect
to see you tonight
i am flooded with desire
in those delicious eyes
that luscious smile
of joyous lips and goodness
you are a beautiful golden orb
of scrumptious desire
i could stand here all night
stare in your eyes
soaking in your soul
all its wondrous joy
tell me love
did you come here for me
you're touching me
i am nervous
what to say next
you end this debate
as you lean in and kiss me

one for you and i

romance novels, love letters and the next step
a day after i got to play mom as a dad
i was wondering how you and the girls are
wondering how you can be
into romance novels
yet not write me back
a hand crafted letter of love
i wonder what you think is so different
than those romance novels
it is so very classic from my perspective
the beautiful girl who wants something she reads
the dashing man who tries to give it to her
it almost sounds so storybook
considering our lives and our girls
i learned long ago
storybooks are the realm of imagination
i am trying to write one for you and i
because i am that kind of man
i thought you were that kind a lady
i want redemption in my life
more than i want the pain of memory
almost as much as i want your love
to drip upon my soul
shower the girls with joy
so everyone is jealous
they see us hand in hand
all smiles and sappy wonder
we gaze into each others eyes
maybe next time i see you
i will just walk up and kiss you
you would know it then
all i want is to love you

not a single flower

not a single flower to pick
i went to make your day
but found that on my walk
i could not find a single flower
to pick and give you
so when i wrapped on your door
that hard knock of my knuckles
i was empty handed in my quest
to let flowers win your heart
i know i must win you with words
that back up my actions
for it is words that you have feared
built your wall around
i should win you with a hammer
i can use to chip the rock wall you built
around that pretty little heart of yours
i sit here smirking though
to know i am an artist through and through
i am selfish with my feelings
because emotion is the energy of my art
the fuel of my mania
even if we are able to meet somewhere
in the middle of our lives
where my flowery words
your delicious beauty
seep into each others soul
what would stop us from our past
that reads more like a tragedy
than a happy ending

with this love song

-

another kiss is right on
as i was laying in bed last night
thinking of your words
the fluttered approach
of the nighttime frogs descended
i could hear their serenade
wondered how i sounded to you
with this love song i keep writing for you
i know i will see you next week
i could not help but wish
the sound of your voice was something
i could hear now
the touch of your skin
that luscious canvas
could be something i could feel now
listening to your voice in my head
i wish next week was here
you snuggled up to me
as our bodies entwined
in the saturation that is
the inevitable outcome
of a love song for an inked doll

redheads, blondes, brunettes and bombshell hooligans

just a laugh for the days
when in my bombastic mood
of sunshine and perfect maze
the bombshell hooligans
are all blondes and brunettes
when you crave a redhead
or vice versus depending on the
temperature of the day
it is just that i want
a compatriot to follow me down
these hooligan shenanigans
i find myself in
it is just that i want
something i am not allowed
you love are so very beautiful
in this noon day sun
your vintage style a gorgeous dress
we should slip off
frolic in the grass
under this noon day sun
where the bombshell hooligans
are all blondes and brunettes
all i crave is a redhead
with ruby lips to kiss

silence and exuberance are a visceral experience

you do not see but the two speeds i run at
when everyone is around or it is just you and i
i crave the luxury of creation
no one sees the rest of me
even when i crave that comfort
it is strangers where i might find
a little respite from within
i do not want to accept this next step
i need you to do it
make this happen for me
for us
i must confess cultivate it
the allure i crave in you
this is a done deal
no matter what
we do and say
it could be epic
a story no one would believe
its one that you live in infamy

the opposite of a rainbow

for so long i did the best i could
i was not in love
not till you were gone
then i remembered
i loved another, and she
well she was always elegant
in those clothes
today is for you
the love i could not pursue
it is so natural for me and you
now that i am free
where are you?

expressing my dissatisfaction

express your disbelief, your sorrow, your frustration
you said this somewhere in a dream
it always seems like i am in a dream of late
this state where i am disconnected
from any reality that is shared with anyone
it takes a while to bleed
the poison from your soul
or so i imagine
because even here with you
i feel no connection to you
other than this silence
i cannot express my feelings for you
in anything other than smiles
a subtle touch
a set of words
my attention for you
it takes a while to bleed the poison out
dissatisfaction is hard to swallow
until there is freedom of choice
then love we need to realize
the rest is up to words
express what you must
i will accept you

self absorbed aggrandizing hooligan

the day, left over from a night
not quite left behind in my thoughts
peoples words can leave a mark
i woke happy to know
what i did and did not do
by the time i was in the studio
i was self absorbed
not even the knowledge of seeing you
could shake this focus on creation
i just needed to be alone
though i tried and tried to paint
my way to some form of realization
in this i am passing through
i know what comfort i do
i wish i could recognize
part of the continuum
i am stuck on
in a moment
i realize i am going through
something profound
i know what i do
it is something you cannot hide
the nefarious character life
i thought you would like it
i wanted you too

the ink pinup couple

i thought you would like to know
there is this image i have of you
in your white slip and black fishnets
you are fixing your garter
as you sit on the edge of the bed
i am standing in the hall, watching
i can see the definition in your calf
your hand runs up your thigh
i can tell you know i am watching
as you pull your slip up
your inner thigh screaming at me
i walked into the room to stand next to you
you look up and smile at me
you spread your legs wider
your white slip shows me
all of your garter straps
i place my fingertips on your shoulder
at the tip of your red star
trace my finger down your arm
till i meet the pinup couple
on your forearm
you and me
we are perfect in ink and life
i lean down kiss your neck
to start your engine
your sexy legs
all dolled up in fishnets
we are not going to make it to the show
you look up at me
with that knowing smile
i love to devour in a kiss

tonight i say goodbye . tomorrow hello love

what can i say to you
other than it may be time
we quit all this silent dancing
begin the conversation in our lives
i keep shooting and writing
working towards this goal
that leads to the adoration of the famous
i wish you were here to help me with it
so we could enjoy the rise together
in envy and adoration the famous preside
this inked doll is more than my lover
she is my beloved
we are on this path in parallel
i keep thinking
if i can jump these tracks
someday i can make it your way
this touch i dream of late at night
as we lay curled in a dream of white
a scrumptious delight
of the sensual love
i believe exists in you
for only me

golden orgasms taste like chocolate

there is nothing but naked skin
my head is resting on your thigh
your hand combing through my hair
a deep satisfying smile on your lips
the scent of your sex pheromones surround us
i can feel that sticky nature on my lips
your voice is so soothing in the space between us
i hear that melody of love in you
i can hear your golden orgasms in my head
this smile is more like pure joy
it is your melody i want to sing again and again
the memory of your labia on my lips
this taste like chocolate
is better than i can imagine
you are better than i can dream
yes i am going to pleasure your ink
your hand in my hair a caressing reminder
of the luscious pleasure in caring how you kiss

this love affair

sometimes my love affair is only
this obsession i have
with creating my art
it cannot be destroyed or even slowed down
at this stage a compulsion is but the gift
to the entropic absorbed world
i wanted only for you to join me
in this trek
hold my hand
walk beside me
trumpet the horn that is me
i know there is no room beside me
not because of ego or the misshapen size
of my alter ego's obsession
this artistic compulsion
can only move forward
at mach 5 much of the time
energy consuming all around me
this needy energy can create
this love affair is over
the moment you could see
i did not control the light switch
the moment you knew
i was in love with you
you would not be second best
in this love affair
it is just that you
would not be the center
of the great i am
rather this art that is a creationists love affair
cannot be replaced by ink on skin
only acrylics on canvas
words on paper
emulsion on film

a flower inside you

having met "the beatnik" last night
i am not sure where or how to connect
that sprite old fella to the modern version in me
i can also see why you say this city is incestuous
your group of friends is incestuous
in the way they sleep with each other
i find it a little bit brash the way they brag about it too
like it's something worth celebrating
coming from a whoring braggadocio like myself
this may be strange
yet i never chased my friends ladies
it's a perk of mine to be the alpha male
to blend with every social circle
it makes it easy to have a variety
an array of talented skirt to choose from
i do not always choose the first floozy
that sniffs around
my tastes are more discriminating
i want you to tantalize my mind
as well as my body
a pretty face just won't do
i interrupted something you said to imply
your motives are similar to mine
i am happy to feel the inspiration
to write these words to you
my love song
in the off chance they awaken
a flower inside you

modern ink style

the old codger at the bar
with grey hair and faded skin
all wrinkles and crazy head boppin
the honky tonk music
a soothing toe tap for him
it's rockabiliy twang night
rocking modern ink style
i am just here to watch this whole little show
having found myself right talking to the man
who drew your attention away from me
it's all smiles for knowing this
all those months before
i like him
there is such a strong assurance
knowing i am always the better man
despite what you do
it is my acceptance of you
i can see you do not recognize
i would remind you
i got the story
i told the stories
we talked of my blonde whore on your day
my drunkard faded memory of what really happened
i guess i do not care where this ends
i am just happy i started it
i am just happy i love you

a story of you

this classic event
in the dirty neon bar
where so much is written
the olympian is a kelly's original
where they used to hang
the original art of roger atkinson
its a dive bar
with inked dolls galore
my kind of scene
there is a subtle sophistication
in a place like this
it's a gritty urban decay
of barflys and alienated youth
that creates this air
of i don't give a fuck
i may be one of the only ones
who celebrates it
the rest here must feel it
it strikes me as the copper top shines
eighties rock blares all around us
i just keep watching you my dear
with all that delicious ink
it looks like fresh acrylics on canvas
i think of what
you would taste like
how touching your skin
would be a delight beyond belief
to trace your art
find my pleasure
your satisfaction
it is this music that makes me smile
i want this to be the start
a moment to remember
when it was a look
we both knew
led to love
your pleasure
my smile
the exploration of skin

is fresh art
like my acrylics on canvas
your skin is my play ground
we explore this beginning
come here and kiss me
let me say i love you
in doing so i will admit
i am lost in this sea
with no plan to make it to shore
i am going to float here
waiting for you
in this turbulent water
where i have no future or past
i exist for you my dear
where the ink like fresh acrylics
painted on blank canvas
these layers a story of you and me
before there was an us
before there was a love song
i sang to you
my beloved inked doll
art is the beautiful spell we release
when we are not looking at each other
in this crowd that does not know
we are divine

more than the ink

today i took a walk on the waterfront in the summer sun
i sat on the grassy knoll we explored that night
after all those crazy encounters
mixed drinks over mixed emotions
it was not our first time to satisfy each other
it is a moment of love i like to remember
like all of my moments with you
this simple fact is a design
to this entropic universe
we understand
it's dive bars and strippers
beers and cigarettes
ink and fishnets my love
for you i sing in the mornings
after we spent the night saturated in skin
i know this love is much more
than the ink on your skin
i have traced like a memory
it is more than fresh acrylics on blank canvas
i paint red roses and orange popsicles
to remind you
there is no greater love than mine
it keeps me warm
on cold lonely nights in the rose city
when they kick us to the curb to smoke a fag
it's such a prude nation we live in my dear
i am not sure they can handle
a pair of punk love birds
like you and i

like there is no tomorrow

drinking tall boys
mighty pints of pabst
whatever you like
i like my Jamesons neat
it's the punk in me
the rose city loves
a celebration
of you and i
we are a pair of lovers
they can sink their teeth into
you a gorgeous inked doll
me an artist with a love affair
the whole world loves to watch
i know these genes
this propensity are all i know
i am very thankful my dear
you celebrate debauchery too
it would break my heart to know
the love of my life
is a storybook unto herself
do you see this endeavor as me
you know i am who i am
i know you are who you are
we celebrate each other
like there is no tomorrow
yet tomorrow dawns like today
all i can say to you
is this love song
is my expression to you

beers like poems

these beers are like poems i write to you
in the times we are not together
a topical glaze so you remember
all that is me
all that is you and i together
i can feel your skin on mine
as you lay your hand on my shoulder
despite you are not here
maybe it is all in memory
banked away
for times like this
when you sat next to me
those eyes of lust and love
i long to see respond to me
as i seek approval in your kisses
touches from your lips
it is only you and i love
on nights like these
with drunkards and meth addicts
playing video crack
all around me
i love the sound of dirty whores
trying to make their way in the night
surrounded by harlequin bums

i paint for you

i am entertaining everyone
at the bar
like we always do
sitting here telling stories
of a poets conquest
defying the established world
its status quo
i wish you were here with me
to show these squares
what it means
to be punk in a dive sitting
to just be alive like the days
we spent in that vegas oasis
with the empty bottles
wet skin
i love the way you kiss
in the warm dry air
after the heat of the sun
runs us inside
to find that pleasure
we both crave
i know the curve of your skin
in the sun
after a long day
of loving you like there is no tomorrow
the heat is a pleasure
of wet ink on skin
like all the canvas'
i paint for you

as good as

i hope my love you feel as good as i do
in whatever dive bar drunk state you are in
know i am there with you
as i sit here tonight
in this dark bar as divvy as they come
drunk and delighted to know
i am myself again
i sing this song to you
in the night
to remember
why i love you doll
it's nights when we are apart
that remind me
of the nights
we have spent together
your pheromone intoxication to me
like a bottle of Jamesons drank straight
as i paint a massive canvas
you are the art i seek
in these long waking nights
when mania wants to take me unaware
i can imagine i was created to love only you
is this any different
than meeting old friends
on a random evening
in my favorite rose city

under neon lights

watching you lean against that golden bar
the hue of your skin under neon lights
i am reminded of all the scrumptious nights
i watched you work your magic on me
felt your magic on me all night
like a soothing balm in mid-winter
when there are no good times outside
i know now like you knew then
this affair is a song of love
we sing to drive the blues away
when we no longer fear
the morning comes swiftly
with the sun and rain of greyscale skies
she looks at him the way
i like when you look at me
it is almost perfectly divine
with all those sweet smiles
the joy you bring
our anticipation
for the pleasure enjoyed later

of self evident prose

today's memory is pumpkin chowder
in a coastal town in october
we are the divine lovers
in this song of songs
like no other written
today or ever sense
i know i do not have to say
i love you
those words hold
a bit of self evident prose
for this love song
i sing to you
my beloved inked doll
in all your sexy glory
i have traced your divinity
on painted skin
like fresch colors
on a blank canvas
how else i express
this feeling i have of you

hoping i see you

this golden hue has the shine of you
a luster brilliantly scuffed and used
it's the perfect surface to explore love
just another dive bar
we spent time in each other
i can hear your laughter above the din of crack
drunks who have been waiting for this all day
i know i have   and
in this bar where memories of you
exist
i want to write your love song again
like its the first time
like all those nights of staring
into your milky pools of lust
memorizing the faces you make to my stories
my touch the memory of fingers
on skin like paint of canvas
the blue plate special tonight is pabst and cigarettes
with a side of nostalgia
i am hoping i see you tonight love
so i can say these words again
in a way you know i love you
this song you already know is yours
this song i sing in the day to remember
this song i sing at night
to cherish our love of debauchery
you and i are meant to dance together
through this life in art
creation on canvas is an exploration in skin
a luscious endeavor we both crave
you, my beautiful inked doll
a woman so perfect i can write this song too
all the world will read it over and over again
all the women will be jealous to know
one man feels so strong in his love for you

pheromone wonderland kisses

so many days and so many nights
fuel the dreams of you and i
on a sunday morning
when the weather keeps us in bed
your legs entwined in mine
our bodies seek the warmth of pleasure
i trace my fingers along your skin
from your calf to your waist
i pause running circles
around your ink
i can smell the pheromones left
from our night of pleasure
the warmth of your sigh
the taste of your soft lips
i can see the love in your eyes
feel the world surround us as we lay in bliss
spooning the morning away
our love a perfect pleasure
your skin
a wonderland of pleasure
a dream i express in words
when i whisper in your ear
in anticipation of your kisses

more to you

i heard the sound
as it escaped your voice
i saw your face
a few moments later
so i smiled at you
knowing there would be more
it is more than touch
it is all about pleasure
i want more of this
beautiful
it is very beautiful in you
you love me more than i know
in all the moments i can wish
the hue of your voice
the pitch of your skin
is more to you than i
this scripture
more than skin and touch
more than voice and love
i will take it all now
today and tomorrow
it is very beautiful in you
when i hear sound from your lips
more to you than love

as almost lovers

i took that leap you asked of me
a subtle flick of divinity
the time was gone and done
with nothing left between
except wonderful memories of lust
i smile like no tomorrow
remembering the times
spent hand in hand
as almost lovers
tomorrow is today is next week as it is last year
the other side looks cleaner
after the grit of brick and mortar
i know so many things about myself
i believe so many things about you
i can say they may not meet
as my almost lover
tomorrow the adventure is lighted
by the hope of all the tomorrows in between
i took the leap you asked me too
i wish you had jumped with me
then this grassy field would be ours
as lovers picking flowers

i know why

i know why you swoon
in the light of day while reading my words
i know why you swoon
in the din of darkness expecting the attention
on you like a warm salve
all this attention is intoxicating
to you and me
in this world where most do not care
in this world where people are cruel
its cold
the way we crush spirits
i know why you swoon
for hope it may bring
to your desolate heart
starved and stammering
for the warmth of love
i know why
i know why you run
after all that swooning
the attention is on you
it feels different
the spotlight of words and love
it feels different
to react to attention
that has a real person behind it
i know why you swoon
i know why you run
i know why the world is cold
why we are at once hot like ice
it comes down to touch
and i know why

the latitude of our sunshine

the latitude of our sunshine
is found in the memories of you and i
pursuing our love song in dive bars
throughout this bitter country
despair in desolate places
we crave the comfort of strangers
clinging to each other
with a wanderlust
that is a moist folly
in between is something else
something known but never spoken
the latitude of our sunshine
is nights riding home
head on shoulder in dirty cabs
driven by mad russians
dirty hipsters
as drunk as we are in each other
there is only tomorrow like today
the latitude of our sunshine
is all about love
a love of you
for me
this is why it begins
where it will end
the latitude of our sunshine
is a story of you and i
a love affair
for our emo selves

i know what you did

there is a pattern i keep seeing
it is never spoken of
not a single word said
except the one time you said to me
i would not hold it against you
its not quite a smile on my face
thinking
i am not the one with the pattern
i am not the one this time
there is a pattern i keep seeing
i wonder if you see it too
if you even know
how it makes me feel
to not ever say a thing
i would not hold it against you
except that it is hidden
subversive
time spent upfront
making it ok
by separation
time spent upfront
separating you from me
subversive and derisive
just to absolve
i see a pattern and i
i know what you did
it would be ok
if you knew
how it makes me feel
time spent upfront
being subversive

joy match up

the time comes quickly
when you and i
will stare
at each other
smile again
for this love that burns
like a flame enriched
with oxygen
it burns brightest
when together
eats at us
when apart
this affair may be perfect
in a time
place we coexist
it has passion
care and kinky love
when apart
its like we do not know
there is another to love
this idea of a we
is the difference between
you and me
like no other
like no other
we are going to
love each other
like no other
before or since
is there enough fuel
to fan the fire
when we are apart
there is a fickle need
one of us will have
that makes it so easy
to walk away
it is ever so perfect
love
to meet your match

to feel your joy
to be lifted up
love
you are a joy to me
i really wish to see
feel breathe
your touch as salvo
in the days of our time
together i want you
my love
to share my life
to be my hope
help create our dreams

i wrote to you

details dear
its always the details
between us that matter
you are alone
i am alone
i crave you
two thousand miles away
i am at the bar
smiling at kelly or tina or tommy
all my favorite bartenders
i am finishing the book
i wrote to you
before i knew you
were more than my hallucination
i wish you were here
so i could make you happy
show you happy
i love
so much more
than you can image
it is real
to believe in me
i believe in you
in spite of you
you deserve it
i am in love
with you
i am in love
with me and the way
i wish you would love me
fear killer
it taints a beautiful soul
like you

to sleep next

the time is shorter
when i am in the west
you in the east
is it sunny there love
it's pissing rain
in the mossy city
where you saw three roses
i am going to smile
because i want to believe
you can love me like i do
i am going to laugh
because i know it makes
you smile
i know you are in a dive bar
like me
this is comfortable for us
it brings me comfort to think
the beautiful you exists
for only me to love
for only me to cherish
will you, won't you
i say yes
i say yes
i do i do i do
either in clevo
the rose city
or somewhere sunny warm
i want to be your love
for all your time
every day
wake up to your smile
to say i am devoted
to you
to sleep next to your
saturated skin
i loved
like no other

just the bliss

it may be late
or early depending
how you define it
i didn't think
i would be up
alone
on a day like this
i am here
in just the bliss
of feeling you
so far away
i think
i am different
for knowing you
for believing in you
for wanting something more
from my self
from my life
i know you are different
from who i met
not who i love
acceptance is my gift
among many i can give you
just the bliss
of knowing your smile
is a warmth
is a light
to shine on this
dark morning
when i cannot tell
is it early or late
where you are
i wish i could
touch you, hug you
kiss you
smile
for the warmth
is just the bliss
of our love

dipole moments

you and i
are dipole moments
that need a magnetic field
to align our love
the space between us
is miles long
measured in thousands
not inches
where i can touch
your wonderful skin
stare into your beautiful eyes
find solace in your love
this charged dipole
craves your touch
needs the love
only you can give me
i want your arms around me
your kisses on my skin
i crave your love
brings me joy

there is tomorrow

i can only smile
for knowing
the cardinal rule
i can only laugh
for hearing
those selfish words
i can only love
for you
the way i know
i can only say
to me
own your feelings
i can only say
to you
there is tomorrow
the end and beginning
are found in the same
creation
all the moments
i know this love
i own this emotion
i believe this future
i see your faults
i know my faults
i own this emotion
i love my future
i love myself
i love you
all the good and bad
i own this self
unlike you
there is tomorrow
in our future

all those nights

i want to smoke and drink
the night away with you
like we did in so many dive bars
across the city
those late nights
of telling stories and laughing
your skin an ever present allure
the link to your ink
all those nights
we spent together
trying to find pleasure
in this love affair
we both decided
is more about you or me
the late nights
in the back of a cab
your skin in my hand
that luscious smile
a milky pool
to lose myself in
as i did
so many times
you are so easy
to love
be lost in

Words of Praise for Lucas Klesch's first poetry book entitled Manic Rose City and first published by Sunshine Ink in 2006.

The Danger
"With cool phrases like 'Brutal Blues' and 'Leaves of Industry,' Manic Rose City evokes imagery like Bob Dylan's in Blonde on Blonde."

"I love the abstract phrasing, disco lemonade, vigilante art, etc. Those are the kinds of phrases that really kick a reader in the nuts, makes 'em think a little in different ways, and opens up ideas and possibilities."

Juan Valdez
"The work, I see and read as lyrics to songs like Steely Dan's hopped up on a Jazzy Rock style!"

Available for purchase at Amazon, Barnes and Noble and other fine bookstores everywhere.

Manic Rose City is a roller coaster ride fun house look at the ups and downs of an artist in the rose city, Portland Oregon. It's a world of denizens and hipster characters, each having a distinguishing name for amusement and notoriety. Manic Rose City is the emotional story spoken in vivid Technicolor of the lyrical nature of living an artist's life. It encompasses all the denizen characters who occupy the life and nightlife of this vibrant rose city. Rich with culture, a strong artists colony, and an independent identity, these poems explore all the important themes of life through an emotional fabric of hills and valleys. The poetry is always following some undercurrent of energy in this manic city and is rich with vibrant manic artistic living. The Frësch Klesch guides us to the characters of the rose city in recurring themes of love, lust, joy and sorrow. The poetry in Manic Rose City is ripe with poignant messages of urban living, human decay, and how there is still a magical place where city dwellers live. Artists consider it their playground where voyeurs love to visit. This book illustrates how an artist struggles with his creative energies, yet is hopelessly full of joy and hope for futures yet explored. It is a compelling tale of love, lust and why poets often are found in bars drinking whiskey on your Tuesdays.

ISBN-10: 097685600X
ISBN-13: 978-0976856009

Words of Praise for Chasing Skirt:

The Sweet Pinkham
"These words are a truth and an anthem of why he chases and why he loves the women he does. Fantastic Delight!."

Azure
"Chasing Skirt is even better than his first book, richer and more livelier in its depth and wonder. The modern phasing is so dynamic in its borderline new divinity that we are compelled to see this world in such gritty modern terms that we can only love the experience of it."

The Danger
"Wicked Cool! The juxtaposition of words and phrases in Chasing Skirt rival no other and truly speak to a new voice in modern punk literature. "

Chasing Skirt is the manifesto of a national past time for an artist as he explains the reasons for his joyous pursuit of women. This pursuit of decadence in a modern adult world of dive bars, Pabst Blue Ribbon and delicious inked dolls weaves a punk cadence of luscious words and science juxtaposed to physical pleasure. His words are an audible delight and ruminating playground that give us an idea of how a woman's essence may taste from the perspective of an artistic life motivated by love and creativity. The Fresch Klesch gives us another look at his dynamic style of describing this raw exploration of his love life. Chasing Skirt is a retrospective look at the reasons why he pursued the relationships in Manic Rose City and how this motivation plays out in his art.

ISBN-10: 0-9768560-1-8
ISBN-13: 978-0-9768560-1-6

Made in the USA
Monee, IL
06 December 2020